GCSE AQA English Language
Spoken Language
Study and Practice Book

This book is for anyone doing
GCSE AQA English Language at foundation level.

It's a **step-by-step guide** to becoming an expert on the Unit 3 Part C
Spoken Language Study controlled assessment.

It's got **everything you need** — study notes, worked examples, practice questions,
practice examples and an assessment-focused guide to analysing
spoken language — to help you get **the grade you want**.

It's ideal for use as a classroom study book
or a revision guide.

What CGP is all about

Our sole aim here at CGP is to produce the highest quality
books — carefully written, immaculately presented and
dangerously close to being funny.

Then we work our socks off to get them out to you
— at the cheapest possible prices.

CONTENTS

Section Four — Multi-Modal Talk

Section Five — The Controlled Assessment

Published by Coordination Group Publications Ltd.

Editors:
Claire Boulter
Polly Cotterill
Edmund Robinson

Produced with:
Alison Smith
Nicola Woodfin

Contributors:
Tony Flanagan
Jan Greenway

With thanks to Heather Gregson and Elisabeth Sanderson for the proofreading.

ISBN: 978 1 84762 547 2

Groovy website: www.cgpbooks.co.uk
Jolly bits of clipart from CorelDRAW®
Printed by Elanders Hindson Ltd, Newcastle upon Tyne.

Based on the classic CGP style created by Richard Parsons.

How to Use This Book

This book will help you with the <u>spoken language</u> controlled assessment for <u>Unit 3 Part C</u> of the <u>AQA English Language GCSE</u>. It's worth <u>10%</u> of your <u>overall mark</u>, so you'd be a fool not to get it in the bag.

Here's what you *Need* to be able to *Do...*

1) Understand <u>how</u> and <u>why</u> people speak <u>differently</u> in different <u>situations</u>.
2) Look at how <u>real-life speech</u> varies between different <u>people</u>, <u>social groups</u> and <u>regions</u>.
3) Understand people's <u>attitudes</u> to different types of speaking.

Each *Section* looks at a *Different Part of Spoken Language*

1 <u>Section One</u> gives you a brief intro on how to study <u>spoken language</u>.

2 <u>Section Two</u> looks at different <u>dialects</u> and how people <u>feel</u> about different <u>types</u> of spoken language.

Alfonso couldn't work out whether the bull was reacting to his spoken language or his dress sense.

3 <u>Section Three</u> gets into different <u>genres</u> (types) of spoken language — e.g. <u>public talk</u>, <u>TV</u> and <u>radio</u>.

4 <u>Section Four</u> is about <u>multi-modal talk</u> — e.g. <u>texting</u>, <u>instant messaging</u> and <u>emails</u>.

<u>Sections Two to Four</u> contain the following stuff to turn you into a spoken language <u>expert</u>:
- Some <u>information</u> about the topic.
- <u>Examples</u> of some spoken language <u>data</u>, showing you the factual stuff in action.
- Some <u>practice questions</u> so you can check that you've understood the topic.

5 <u>Section Five</u> tells you how to do well in the <u>controlled assessment</u>.

It's English, Jim, but not as we know it...
So, your work for this unit is almost certain to include watching TV, texting your mates or playing around in chat rooms. Put like that, it doesn't sound too scary, does it...

Introduction to Spoken Language

Unlike written language, <u>spoken conversations</u> are normally <u>unplanned</u> and <u>unpredictable</u>.

There are lots of Different Types of Spoken Language

It's <u>easier</u> to study <u>spoken language</u> if you can get it down in <u>writing</u>. For example:

- <u>Transcript</u> — this is when <u>speech</u> (e.g. a conversation between two people) is written down.
- <u>Script</u> — this is when language is <u>written</u> down in order to be <u>spoken</u>, e.g. a TV script.
- <u>Multi-modal talk</u> — this includes things like <u>emails</u>, <u>instant messaging</u> and <u>text messaging</u>.

- This is the kind of stuff you'll be looking at for your <u>controlled assessment</u>.

No, not that. <u>THIS</u>.

Listen out for Sounds, Vocabulary and Grammar

There are <u>three</u> main things to listen out for when you <u>analyse spoken language</u>:

1) How the language sounds
- How the speaker <u>pronounces</u> words might tell you something about <u>where</u> they're from.
- It might also tell you about their <u>social background</u> — e.g. that they're middle class.

2) The speaker's vocabulary (the words they use)
- Some words are only used in certain <u>places</u>.
- People's vocabulary <u>changes</u> according to <u>who</u> they're talking to, e.g. you probably use more <u>slang</u> when you talk to your mates than when you talk to a teacher.

3) The speaker's grammar
- <u>Non-standard grammar</u> gives you clues about <u>where</u> the speaker's <u>from</u>.
- E.g. lots of dialects in the <u>north</u> of England use 'he were' rather than 'he was'.

Eee, that were reet interesting...
Who knew you could tell so much about a person just by looking at how they talk. It makes me a bit paranoid, actually. That's why I've adopted a fake Yorkshire accent, just in case they're watching me...

Speech Features

The next few pages are an <u>intro</u> to the things you need to listen out for in <u>conversations</u>.

People <u>Usually try to be</u> Polite <u>to each other</u>

There are different ways of making sure that you <u>don't fall out</u> with the people you're talking to:

Feedback

This is when you say things like '<u>yeah</u>' or '<u>mm</u>' to show someone you're <u>listening</u> to them.

Pragmatics

- These are the <u>hidden</u> or <u>suggested meanings</u> of what people say.
- E.g. you might say to a friend "This maths homework's impossible", when what you <u>mean</u> is "Can you help me with it?".

Language <u>Changes depending on</u> Who <u>you're talking to</u>

If someone says "Open that door", they're probably talking to someone they <u>know well</u> or are <u>in charge of</u>.

But, if they say "I'm sorry, but would you mind opening the door?" they're probably talking to someone <u>important</u> or someone they <u>don't know very well</u>.

What people <u>call</u> each other can also tell you a lot about who has the <u>power</u> in their <u>relationship</u>. For example, you'd probably call your headmaster 'sir' rather than 'mate'.

People <u>Talk Differently</u> in <u>Different Situations</u>

1) You can tell <u>where</u>, <u>when</u> and <u>why</u> a conversation is taking place.
2) E.g. when you're paying for something in a shop you'll probably use <u>set phrases</u> like '<u>there you go</u>' and '<u>thanks</u>'.

Where? When? Why oh why?

People talk differently if they're holding a puppet too...

When studying spoken language is new to you, there's a lot to take in, so make sure it all makes sense by listening to conversations and trying to pick out some of the things on this page.

Speech Features

Spoken language <u>isn't</u> all about words. The odd <u>hand gesture</u> can change their whole <u>meaning</u>.

Spoken Language *is different from* Written Language

When people are speaking <u>naturally</u>, they <u>interrupt</u> each other and <u>stumble</u> over their words.
These are called <u>non-fluency features</u>. Here are some examples:

Non-fluency features

- <u>Fillers</u> (e.g. 'er', 'um') — these <u>fill gaps</u> while the speaker thinks of what they want to say.
- <u>False starts</u> — where the speaker starts saying one thing, then <u>changes their mind</u> and says something else, e.g. 'it doesn't always it doesn't do that very often'.
- <u>Repetition</u> — people repeat words a lot in unplanned speech, e.g. 'I'm never never going'.
- <u>Interruption/overlap</u> — people <u>talk over</u> each other because it's not always clear when someone's finished, or because they're showing that they <u>agree</u> or <u>disagree</u>.

Other features

- <u>Missing words</u> — e.g. 'want to come out' instead of '<u>do you</u> want to come out'.
- <u>Slurring words together</u> — e.g. 'gonna' instead of 'going to'.
- <u>Small talk</u> — phrases that don't have much <u>meaning</u>, e.g. 'Hi, how are you?', or 'Bye'.
- <u>'Vague' language</u> — e.g. saying 'sort of', 'like' or 'lots'.
- <u>Turn-taking</u> — speakers take it in turns to lead the conversation.

Spoken Language *isn't just about* Words

The <u>features</u> of speech <u>that aren't words</u> — e.g. <u>hand gestures</u> and <u>tone of voice</u>, can <u>change</u> the <u>meaning</u> of what you're saying:

- <u>Stress</u> — <u>emphasising</u> certain words can change the <u>meaning</u> of the sentence.

- <u>Tone</u> — <u>how</u> something is said (e.g. someone's tone could be <u>playful</u> or <u>serious</u>).

- <u>Volume</u> — e.g. <u>loudness</u> might show <u>anger</u>, <u>excitement</u> or <u>confidence</u>.

I'm bilingual — I'm fluent in English and body-language...
Warning: Make sure you know exactly what you're doing before you go around throwing any wild hand gestures — vases, ornamental teapots and human eyeballs are often very hard to replace.

Speech Features

Safety goggles on, it's <u>transcript</u> time. These are absolute <u>gold</u> when you're <u>analysing spoken language</u>.

Transcripts are Really Useful for spoken language study

Recordings of speech can be <u>transcribed</u> (written down) to make them <u>easier to study</u>.

1) You might see transcripts written in <u>different ways</u> in different books, but the basic idea is always <u>the same</u> — write down <u>exactly</u> what you hear.
2) We've written down <u>everything</u> the speakers say, including 'filler' words like 'er' and 'um'.
3) We <u>haven't</u> used <u>commas</u>, <u>full stops</u>, <u>question marks</u> etc. Instead, <u>pauses</u> are shown like this:

> **Key**
>
> (.) = <u>micropause</u> (less than 1 second)
>
> (2) = a <u>pause</u> showing the number of <u>seconds</u> it lasts (so this one's <u>2 seconds</u> long).
>
> <u>Interruptions</u> or <u>overlap</u> are shown using the symbol // at the point where someone's interrupted.

So... here's what a <u>transcript</u> of a <u>conversation</u> between <u>two people</u> might look like:

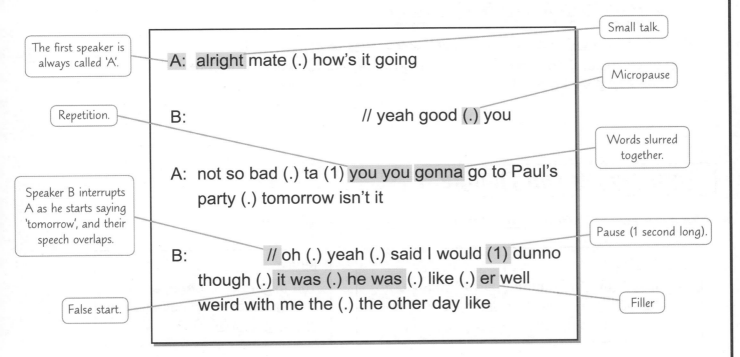

The first speaker is always called 'A'.

Small talk.

Micropause

Repetition.

Words slurred together.

Speaker B interrupts A as he starts saying 'tomorrow', and their speech overlaps.

Pause (1 second long).

False start.

Filler

A: alright mate (.) how's it going

B: // yeah good (.) you

A: not so bad (.) ta (1) you you gonna go to Paul's party (.) tomorrow isn't it

B: // oh (.) yeah (.) said I would (1) dunno though (.) it was (.) he was (.) like (.) er well weird with me the (.) the other day like

What does a tiny dog have at the end of its legs?...

...Micropaws. If you don't get that joke, it's definitely not because it's not funny — you probably just need to read the page again. Oh, well done on getting to the end of Section 1, by the way.

Accent and Dialect

Whether they're from the other side of the world or just up the road, people can <u>sound</u> very <u>different</u>.

Your Accent is How you Pronounce words

1) People with different <u>accents</u> <u>pronounce</u> the same words in <u>different ways</u>.
2) An <u>accent</u> is just <u>how</u> you say words. A <u>dialect</u> is the actual <u>words you use</u>.

Accents depend on Where someone's From...

1) <u>Regional accents</u> are <u>different</u> depending on which part of the country the speaker's from.
2) In <u>England</u>, most people can tell the big differences between <u>northern</u> and <u>southern accents</u>:

> Someone with a <u>northern accent</u> would say '<u>grass</u>' with a <u>short vowel sound</u>, to sound like '<u>cat</u>'.

> Someone with a <u>southern accent</u> would say '<u>grass</u>' like '<u>grarss</u>'.

...and on their Social Background

1) A <u>social accent</u> is the result of someone's <u>class</u> or <u>background</u>.
2) For example, if someone has a really '<u>posh</u>' accent, you can figure out their <u>social background</u>, but you <u>can't</u> tell <u>where</u> they come from.

Your Accent can Change

People's accents might <u>change</u> for different <u>reasons</u>, for example:

<u>Geography</u>	<u>Media</u>
You might <u>move</u> to another part of the country and <u>change</u> your speech to <u>fit in</u>, or so you can be <u>more easily understood</u>.	You might use a <u>stronger</u> regional accent because you're <u>copying people</u> off the **TV**.

Geography can affect speakers — closer people are louder...

Remember that just because people might use different grammar or different words for things, it doesn't mean what they are saying is wrong — they're just showcasing their exotic dialect.

Accent and Dialect

Just a <u>bit</u> more about <u>accent and dialect</u>, and then you're done. See, I told you it wasn't too tricky...

Your *Dialect* is the *Words you use*

1) The word <u>dialect</u> is usually used to describe the language that people use in a <u>certain place</u>, e.g. 'Cornish dialect' is the dialect people use in Cornwall.

2) Dialects have their own <u>words</u>, <u>grammar</u> and <u>pronunciation</u>. For example:

Vocab	Different dialects have different words for things, e.g. in Northern Ireland and Scotland, people say '<u>wee</u>' to mean '<u>little</u>'.
Grammar	Regional dialects contain <u>non-standard</u> grammar, e.g. missing plurals — "it costs four <u>pound</u>" (instead of 'pounds').
Pronunciation	Most regional dialects also have an <u>accent</u> to go with them.

People speak *Differently* in *Different Situations*

1) You might use a <u>different accent</u> or <u>dialect</u> depending on <u>where you are</u> or <u>who you're with</u>.

2) A speaker might use <u>Standard English</u> (see p.10) to make people think they're <u>intelligent</u> or <u>posh</u>.

3) On the other hand, they might use a <u>regional accent</u> or <u>dialect</u> to make them seem more <u>friendly</u> and <u>down-to-earth</u>.

Rupert spoke Standard English to Lily, but never a word to anyone else.

Think about how you speak differently in different situations. For example, you might use <u>Standard English</u> at school, and a <u>regional dialect</u> at <u>home</u>, or the other way round.

You say tomayto — I say tomarto...

Blimey. That bunch of mumbling randomers from the other side of the country seem a bit more complex than I thought, now. Well, there's plenty more where that came from...

Accent and Dialect — Worked Example

As with all of these topics, if you want to write about this in the <u>controlled assessment</u>, you're going to have to be able to <u>analyse</u> some <u>data</u>. Here's an example of the kind of things to look out for. (Have a look at p.5 if you're not sure what the numbers and symbols in the <u>transcript</u> mean.)

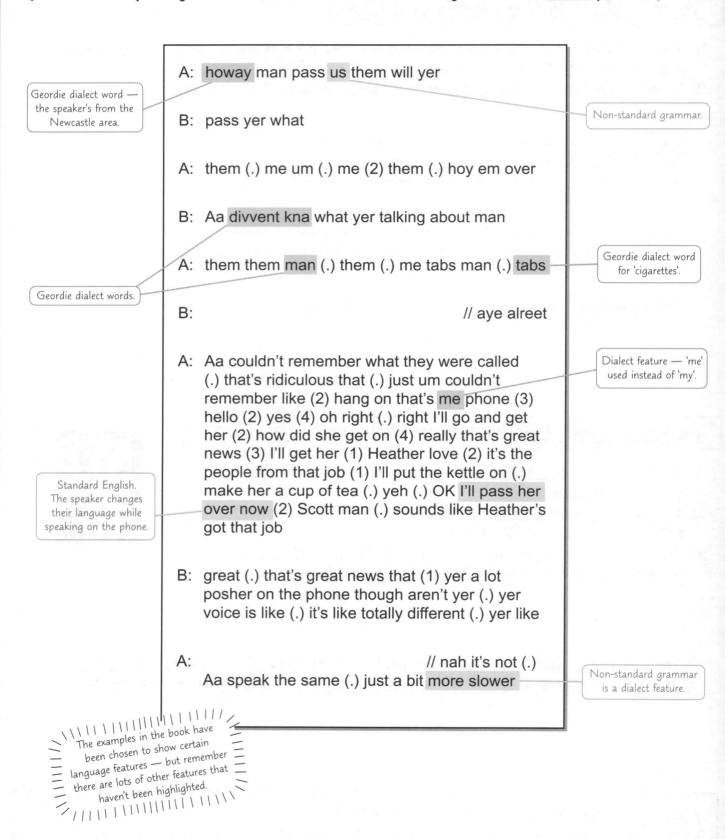

A: howay man pass us them will yer

Geordie dialect word — the speaker's from the Newcastle area.

Non-standard grammar.

B: pass yer what

A: them (.) me um (.) me (2) them (.) hoy em over

B: Aa divvent kna what yer talking about man

A: them them man (.) them (.) me tabs man (.) tabs

Geordie dialect words.

Geordie dialect word for 'cigarettes'.

B: // aye alreet

A: Aa couldn't remember what they were called (.) that's ridiculous that (.) just um couldn't remember like (2) hang on that's me phone (3) hello (2) yes (4) oh right (.) right I'll go and get her (2) how did she get on (4) really that's great news (3) I'll get her (1) Heather love (2) it's the people from that job (1) I'll put the kettle on (.) make her a cup of tea (.) yeh (.) OK I'll pass her over now (2) Scott man (.) sounds like Heather's got that job

Dialect feature — 'me' used instead of 'my'.

Standard English. The speaker changes their language while speaking on the phone.

B: great (.) that's great news that (1) yer a lot posher on the phone though aren't yer (.) yer voice is like (.) it's like totally different (.) yer like

A: // nah it's not (.)
   Aa speak the same (.) just a bit more slower

Non-standard grammar is a dialect feature.

The examples in the book have been chosen to show certain language features — but remember there are lots of other features that haven't been highlighted.

Accent and Dialect — Practice Questions

Accents and dialects are real <u>bread-and-butter</u> stuff so make sure you can handle these questions. If you're <u>struggling</u>, have a <u>look back</u> over the last couple of pages and then give them another go.

Q1   Which of these statements is false? Choose one answer.

   a) Your accent is different depending on where you're from.
   b) Your accent can never change.
   c) Accents are just different ways of pronouncing words.

Q2   What does a social accent tell you about the speaker?

Q3   Name one thing that could cause someone's accent to change.

Q4   What's the difference between accent and dialect?

Q5   Why might someone choose to use a stronger regional accent or dialect?

Standard English

Standard English (SE) is <u>exactly</u> what its name suggests. You should still read the page though...

Standard English <u>is a Social Dialect</u>

<u>Standard English</u> is a <u>dialect</u> of English, like <u>Cockney</u> or <u>Scouse</u>, but it <u>isn't</u> just used in one place.

1) A <u>standard</u> form of a language is the type that people think is <u>acceptable</u> or <u>correct</u> — e.g. what you look up in a <u>dictionary</u> is Standard English.

2) It's used in things like <u>newspapers</u> and <u>formal documents</u>.

3) It's associated with <u>education</u>, <u>class</u> and <u>power</u>, rather than with a particular <u>area</u> of the country.

Standard English: when you haven't got room for the full English.

This Book <u>is written in Standard English</u>

1) If your language gets <u>corrected</u> at school, then that's your teacher asking you to use <u>SE</u>. It's the type of English that seems '<u>proper</u>' or '<u>posh</u>'.

2) Here's an example of the <u>same</u> sentence written in <u>Standard</u> and <u>non-standard</u> English:

Standard grammar.

Standard English word — all English speakers would know what it means.

Standard English: Dad <u>was</u> tired because the <u>children</u> couldn't sleep.

Dialect word — speakers from different areas might not understand it.

Non-standard English: Dad <u>were</u> tired <u>coz</u> the <u>bairns</u> couldn't sleep.

Non-standard grammar.   Non-standard spelling.

<u>It's tricky — but easier than studying Standard Icelandic...</u>
Granted it's a bit of a fiddly one to get your head round at first, but all this stuff on Standard English is easy when you know how. Keep your ears open and see when you can spot it.

Worked Example and Practice Questions

Have a read of this <u>wedding speech</u>, which is written in <u>Standard English</u>. I've pointed out some tasty language features for you to enjoy too. Then see how you get on with the questions.

The speaker doesn't have an obvious regional or social dialect.

Standard vocabulary — traditional way of starting a formal speech.

ladies and gentleman (.) boys and girls (1) as father of the er bride I would like to er (.) to thank you all so very much for coming here today and sharing in this (.) this wonderful occasion (.) the wedding of my dear daughter Claire and her um her handsome young groom (.) Peter (2) I'd also like to thank (.) to thank everyone who played a part in making this day so special (1) um (2) hang on (.) right (.) sorry (1) I'd er (.) first off (.) I'd like to thank er (.) Patrick (.) my er (.) my brother (.) and the rest of the um the committee of the South Riesling Cricket Club (.) for (.) for allowing us to use the this cricket field for the rather um (.) pleasant marquee in which we're gathered (2) similarly (.) I'd like to to thank my sister (.) Eileen (.) for er (.) for organising the beautiful display of er (.) of flowers that you see here today (1) one of the um (.) um (.) advantages of having a florist in the family

Standard vocabulary — instead of a slang word like 'fit' or 'buff'.

Standard grammar.

Q1 What is Standard English?

Q2 Name two situations where people usually use Standard English.

Q3 Which of the sentences below is in Standard English? Choose one answer.

a) You was trying your hardest to catch me.

b) I've only gone and lost my rail card.

c) Ben and Adam's well good at football.

Slang

Slang goes <u>in</u> and <u>out of fashion</u> faster than the shoulder pad, and some of it will keep on cropping up in random places till the end of time. Much like the faithful mullet...

Slang is Informal

1) Slang words are <u>informal</u> and <u>chatty</u>. People use them most in <u>casual speech</u>.

> e.g. *cool* (good), *mare* (nightmare), *yonks* (a long time, ages).

2) People often use slang to sound <u>rebellious</u> or <u>funny</u>, e.g. there's lots of slang about things like <u>sex</u>, <u>sex organs</u> and <u>bodily functions</u>. Tee hee.

Certain Groups have their Own Slang

1) Some slang words are understood pretty much <u>everywhere</u> — e.g. most <u>swear words</u>.

2) Others are <u>specific</u> to certain <u>places</u> or <u>groups of people</u> (e.g. Cockney rhyming slang), so outsiders might have trouble <u>understanding</u> them.

3) The amount of slang you use depends on <u>who</u> you're talking to (e.g. you'd probably use less slang in a <u>job interview</u> than you would if you were just chatting with your <u>mates</u>).

Slang is Always Changing

1) Slang words go in and out of <u>fashion</u> really <u>quickly</u>.

2) They can quickly start to sound <u>dated</u>, e.g. words like 'mega' ('good'), or 'dweeb' (someone who isn't cool).

3) This happens especially with <u>teenage slang</u>. When adults and younger children pick a word up, teenagers stop using it.

Slang will come and go, but it's always good to be cool.

Slang — it's one letter away from a rude example of itself...

Cool beans. Slang constantly adapts and evolves — faster than you can say 'I think slang is pretty radical, far out, bogus, gnarley, zomba, sick, hip, bad, funky, killer-diller, heavy, stellar, tubular...'

Slang — Worked Example

Here's a most enlightening <u>conversation</u> between two lovely young ladies. It's jam-packed full of <u>slang</u>, which I've helpfully pointed out for you. Once you've read it there are some questions too.

The casual language and use of slang show this is a conversation between close friends.

A: hey chica (1) soz I'm late (.) I'm in a total **Mondaze**

Combination of 'Monday' and 'daze'.

B: // chill girl (.) it's no big (1) so (.) come on (.) spill

A: // oh my God (.) so it was like (.) totally bunk (.) we (.) we like rock up at the club and we're (.) he's not even got us on the (.) the guest list (.) so we're like (.) like queuing and some (.) some cow shoves past me (.) right

B: // that's so not cool

'Like' is used a lot as a 'vague' filler.

A: damn straight (.) yeah (.) proper tarty (.) really **minging**

Slang word for 'ugly' or 'gross'.

B: // okay (.) so please tell me Jay at least (.) **like** (.) like fronted her (.) yeah

A: nah (.) that's it (.) loser couldn't take his eyes off her (1) said a girl that **fine** could (.) could do what she (.) what she liked

Slang word for 'attractive'.

B: // ah babe (.) that sucks (1) I mean the (.) guy's fit as (.) but what a (.) a total lamester

A: // I know babe (.) I was like (.) **proper** vexed at him but we (.) I just thought (1) you know (1) whatever (.) am here to to have fun (.) right (.) so I (.) I just went and danced with Carly

Speaker A uses the word 'proper' a lot.

B: was (.) wasn't she with Dan

A: nah (.) he was (.) didn't come in the end (.) he went round Keith's (1) they've got like a (.) a proper **bromance** going on

Combination of 'brother' and 'romance'.

Slang — Practice Questions

Just to keep you on your toes, I thought you might fancy a few <u>practice questions</u> about <u>slang</u> words. See how you get on with these ones. If there are any that you're really struggling with, have <u>another read over</u> the last few pages and give them <u>another go</u>.

Q1   What is slang?

Q2   Give one reason why people might use slang.

Q3   The sentences below mean the same thing. Which one contains slang?

     a)   I'm very well, thanks.

     b)   I'm wicked, cheers.

Q4   Which group of people would you expect to use the most slang?

     a)   work colleagues

     b)   teenagers

     c)   young children

Q5   Why might teenage slang suddenly become unpopular with teenagers?

Language in Groups

Now you've hopefully recovered from all that <u>vile</u> and <u>vulgar</u> slang, here's a lovely page all about language in groups. It sounds as though it should be complicated — but it's actually <u>not too tricky</u>.

Different Groups Speak Differently *from each other*

1) <u>Different groups</u> of people use <u>different language</u> when they're talking <u>together</u>.

2) For example, middle-aged lawyers speak <u>differently</u> from teenagers.

3) <u>Sharing</u> group language gives a group an <u>identity</u> — people use it to <u>fit in</u>.

> For example, groups of young people might speak in a way that older people find <u>hard to understand</u>.

Different Jobs *have their own* Group Language

"Pass the cutter-uppers, I need to make a thingummyjig in the wotsit."

1) People who do the <u>same job</u> often have their own <u>group language</u>. E.g. <u>train drivers</u> use different words at work compared to <u>nurses</u>.

2) It makes communicating at work <u>quicker</u> and more <u>precise</u>.

3) It's made up of <u>jargon</u> — <u>specialist words</u> that people who don't do the job might not understand.

4) E.g. <u>electricians</u> might use words like 'transformer', 'fuse', 'amp', 'earth'.

Men *and* Women *use different* Group Language

1) Studies have shown that <u>women</u> use more <u>Standard English</u> than men.

2) They also <u>swear</u> and <u>interrupt less</u> than men.

3) It seems that <u>men</u> use more <u>non-standard grammar</u> and are more likely to have stronger <u>regional accents</u>.

> IMPORTANT POINT
>
> You should bear in mind that lots of men and women don't fit in with these findings.

Football fans use a very strange group language...

Football jargon words like 'ref', 'offside', 'six-yard-box', 'linesman', 'back-heel', 'bicycle kick' and 'nutmeg' wouldn't make much sense to someone who's never seen a football game in their life.

Language in Groups

It'll be really useful to know about language in groups for your <u>GCSE</u>, and luckily for you, you're on <u>exactly</u> the right page to find out the rest of it. Coincidence? Or fate...

Group Language **also crops up in** Texts **and** Emails

1) You can see group language in <u>multi-modal</u> texts (see section 4), like <u>text messages</u>, <u>emails</u> and <u>instant messenger conversations</u>.

2) Most people write in a <u>similar</u> way to how they <u>talk</u> when they're <u>texting</u> or <u>emailing</u>.

Language Changes **depending on the** Situation **you're in**

1) People use <u>different group language</u> depending on <u>who</u> they're talking to.

2) You might find that the way you speak <u>changes</u> depending on:

- Who you're with — e.g. the language you use with a <u>brother</u> or <u>sister</u> might contain slang that your <u>parents</u> don't understand.

- Where you are — e.g. if you're in a <u>computer shop</u> you'd probably use words like 'RAM' and 'hard drive' that you wouldn't use if you were at the <u>cinema</u>.

- What you're doing — e.g. if you're <u>giving a speech</u> at school you might use more <u>Standard English</u> because you're in a <u>formal situation</u>.

"Howzat!"

Using the right '<u>type</u>' of language in <u>different situations</u> is really important for making yourself understood. E.g. if the <u>newsagent</u> told you to '<u>open wide</u>', you'd think it was pretty <u>weird</u>, but you wouldn't think it was weird at the <u>dentist's</u>...

When I'm eating... my tea... I take longer... pauses...

This stuff on language changing in different contexts is really important as it applies to slang, accent, dialect and group language equally. Hopefully it's all making sense and going in, so far.

Worked Example

If you've read the last couple of pages, you should now be an expert in <u>group language</u>. Make sure you know what it's all about by reading this <u>worked example</u> then having a bash at the <u>questions</u>.

A: right (.) it depends on what kind of exercise you're looking for (1) spinning's a er great workout but it's pretty intense

> Jargon words about fitness and training.

B: yeah (.) I'm a bit out of of shape (.) I'd better start off gentle

A: what d'you do for a living mate

> The speakers both use informal language to seem more friendly.

B: // I'm a er (.) landscape gardener (1) water features and that (.) y'know

> Speaker A interrupts speaker B.

A: // cool (1) must keep you pretty fit (.) yeah

B: used to (.) yeah (.) I'm more on the design side now though (1) where would you like your sun terrace (.) madam (1)

> Speaker B's job jargon is different from speaker A's.

A: // haha (.) yeah (.)

B: // know what I mean

A: yeah (.) well (.) no worries mate (.) we can sort you out (1) I reckon you should start off with boxercise (1) it's great for cardio

> Jargon. Combination of 'boxing' and 'exercise'.

B: yeah (1) well that's um what (.) what I oh boxercise (1) sorry I thought you said exercise (.) haha

A: // haha (.) yeah (.) sorry pal (.) it I guess it is er pretty loud in here (1) yeah (.) boxercise

B: the hearing's not what it what it used to be y'know (.) I um used to play a bit of rugby (.) but I had to erm (.) call it a day cos I couldn't even hear the line-out calls haha

> This is rugby jargon.

Practice Questions

Give these <u>practice questions</u> a shot. This stuff seems simple when you read it on the page, but it's no good to you unless you can <u>understand</u> it and <u>remember</u> it.

Q1   True or false? Group language can give a social group an identity.

Q2 a)   Which of these groups is most likely to have its own way of talking? Choose one answer.

    i)   Patients in a waiting room

    ii) A crowd in a shop

    iii) Friends in the school playground

b)   Give one more example of a group that might have its own way of talking.

Q3   Why do people use jargon at work?

Q4   Apart from in spoken language, where else might you be able to spot group language? Choose one answer.

    a) On a train timetable

    b) In multi-modal texts like emails and text messages

    c) In a recipe book

Idiolect

It's <u>really important</u> to know about <u>idiolects</u> for your GCSE. You'll need to think about how <u>all</u> the little <u>bits and bobs</u> that have come up so far form how <u>one person</u> speaks.

Idiolect *is the* Unique *way a* Person *speaks*

1) The way you use language can be a big part of your <u>identity</u>.
2) Your individual way of speaking is called your <u>idiolect</u>.
3) It's basically the <u>unique combination</u> of all the different things covered in this section, that makes your speech <u>yours</u>.

Idiolect *is Influenced* by *Your Background...*

...the Places *you've* Lived*...*

1) For example, if you're from Plymouth then you might have a West Country <u>accent</u> and use <u>dialect</u> words, like 'bock' for 'mess up'.
2) But not everyone from the same <u>area</u> speaks in exactly the <u>same</u> way.
   E.g. You might have <u>moved</u> from somewhere else and kept some bits from your <u>other</u> regional accent and dialect, while picking up bits of the Plymouth one.
3) This way of speaking will be <u>unique</u> to you.

...and the People *you've* Spent Time With

1) Your <u>social background</u> is also part of your <u>idiolect</u>.
2) The <u>accents</u> and <u>dialects</u> you've had contact with have all had some effect in making you speak the way you do <u>today</u>.
3) Your idiolect <u>doesn't stay the same</u> — it'll <u>change</u> all the time.

Liam's idiolect had changed a lot since he started spending all his time with that horse.

Lloyd Grossman — *now that's an interesting idiolect...*
Your idiolect is basically the result of everything that makes you talk in the way that you do. If you're not too sure about it, have a look at the worked example and questions on page 21.

Idiolect

Who you calling idiolect?! Oh. Oh I see....

__Your Idiolect is also influenced by your Age...__

- __Young people__ often use more __slang__ words (e.g. 'cool', 'lame') than older people.
- A lot of __young people__ use more '__vague__' language (e.g. '__like__' and '__sort of__') than older people.
- So you probably __wouldn't__ hear your __grandad__ saying:
  "It like totally sucked cos I turned to him and was like 'bite me' and he was like 'whatever'."

__...and the Group Language that you use__

1) The way you speak is __influenced__ by all the different __groups__ you're part of, and the __language__ you use in those groups.
2) For example, you might be:

   | middle class __AND__ a teenager __AND__ a football player |

3) __All__ of these things will __affect__ your __idiolect__.

Kenneth's idiolect was calm, soft and strangely flirtatious.

4) Your idiolect also __changes__ depending on the __situation__ you're in — e.g. you might speak differently to a teacher than you do to a friend.

5) The way you __change__ your language when you're with __different people__ or in __different situations__ is called your __repertoire__.
6) Everyone's repertoire is __unique__.

__Old people speak differently — Granny's always swearing...__

There are some tricky words here — things like 'idiolect' and 'repertoire'. If you want to impress the examiner, learn how to spell them and what they mean, then use them in your controlled assessment.

Worked Example and Practice Questions

Have a look at the <u>idiolect features</u> picked out in this worked example, and then try the questions.

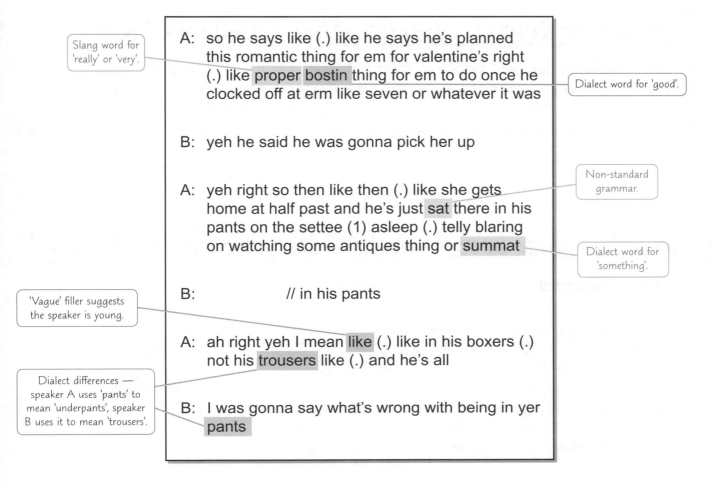

Slang word for 'really' or 'very'.

A: so he says like (.) like he says he's planned this romantic thing for em for valentine's right (.) like proper bostin thing for em to do once he clocked off at erm like seven or whatever it was

Dialect word for 'good'.

B: yeh he said he was gonna pick her up

Non-standard grammar.

A: yeh right so then like then (.) like she gets home at half past and he's just sat there in his pants on the settee (1) asleep (.) telly blaring on watching some antiques thing or summat

Dialect word for 'something'.

'Vague' filler suggests the speaker is young.

B: // in his pants

A: ah right yeh I mean like (.) like in his boxers (.) not his trousers like (.) and he's all

Dialect differences — speaker A uses 'pants' to mean 'underpants', speaker B uses it to mean 'trousers'.

B: I was gonna say what's wrong with being in yer pants

Q1   What is idiolect? Choose one answer.

a)   The unique language of a social group.

b)   The unique language of a geographical region.

c)   The unique language of an individual speaker.

Q2   Which of these things is likely to form part of a teenager's idiolect? Choose one answer.

a)   Cockney dialect words like 'blag' and 'chuffed'.

b)   Jargon words about golf, such as 'birdie' and 'eagle'.

c)   'Vague' filler words such as 'like' and 'sort of'.

Social Attitudes to Spoken Language

The way a person <u>speaks</u> affects what other people <u>think about them</u>.

People have *Different Attitudes* towards *Standard English*

1) Some people see <u>Standard English</u> as '<u>correct</u>' English, so other dialects <u>aren't</u> correct.

2) They might worry about <u>text speak</u> in things like <u>emails</u> and <u>text messages</u> (see section 4) because they think that young people <u>won't know how</u> to use English 'correctly'.

3) Other people argue that language is <u>always changing</u>, so there's no 'right' or 'wrong' way of using it.

You might Judge *people because of their* Accent *and* Dialect

We all make <u>judgements</u> about other people based on how they speak. For example:

1) People from the <u>north</u> of England might think people with <u>southern accents</u> sound '<u>posh</u>'.

2) Some people think that people who use <u>regional dialects</u> are <u>uneducated</u> or <u>lower class</u>.

3) But other people think they sound more <u>friendly</u>. They might think someone's trying to sound 'fancy' if they <u>change</u> their <u>regional dialect</u>.

Terry had a unique way of showing his own social attitudes.

Some people think Slang *is* Incorrect English

Lots of people think <u>slang</u> is too <u>informal</u> to use in certain situations.

1) Some people worry that slang doesn't follow the <u>rules</u> of <u>Standard English</u>.

2) They <u>assume</u> that people who use lots of slang are <u>lower class</u> and <u>uneducated</u>.

3) Slang is seen as <u>informal</u>, so some people think you <u>shouldn't</u> use it in a <u>formal situation</u> — e.g. you'd lose marks if you put lots of slang in an essay.

I don't like your attitude, young lady...

Spoken language is something you'll come across every day including the day of your GCSE, so make sure you know what other people think about it and can talk about their different opinions.

Worked Example

This is the <u>mother of all examples</u>. The next <u>four pages</u> cover examples and questions for everything in Section Two. Dialects, slang, idiolect — the lot. So, deep breath, and here we go...

A: so where does it hurt exactly

'Me' used instead of 'my'. This is non-standard grammar.

B: I think it's one of me (1) me back teeth (2)

Jargon word about dentistry.

A: // I expect it's a molar (1) when did you last have a check-up

The dentist uses Standard English, which suggests he or she is educated and middle class.

B: can't member (3) bout (.) er (.) bout a year ago (.) yeah cos we was (.) going away like

'We was' instead of 'we were'. This is non-standard grammar.

A: well (.) I'll sort this out for you now (6) looks like you'll be needing a (.) a filling

Jargon word about dentistry.

B: // okicoki

Part of the speaker's idiolect, meaning 'OK'.

A: I'll just give you a little injection (.) numb the pain (1) or would you prefer without

Slang term for 'injection'.

B: well (1) I (.) er (.) I think you'd best give us a jab (1) if (.) if it's gonna hurt like

Dialect feature — 'us' instead of 'me'.

Slang word.

A: o(.)kay (2) just hold still for a jiffy and (3) there we go (5) can you feel (1) that

The words 'get it' are slurred together.

B: that's (.) yeah (1) nothing (2) let's geddit over with doc

The dentist tells the patient what to do, which shows that the dentist has power in the conversation.

A: great (2) now (.) just relax (1) you might feel a slight (.) pressure but it (.) it won't hurt a bit

Worked Example

Now have a look at this little lot. By the end of this page you'll be a <u>spoken language machine</u>, able to take over the linguistic world and rule with your mighty tongue. (Small print: this may not actually happen.)

Small talk.

A: Mrs Trafford (.) how are you today (.) sorry to have kept you (1) we've been rushed off our feet all morning (2) now then (.) what can I do for you

B: well (.) I'd like the (.) the back left long (.) but I think perhaps some layers at the top

Jargon words about hairdressing.

A: no probs Mrs Trafford (1) looks like you've got a (.) a few split ends here at the back

Slang word.

B: // oh crikey (1) how awful (1) well just (.) just do as you think best Sandra

Speaker A calls speaker B 'Mrs Trafford', but speaker B calls speaker A 'Sandra'. 'Mrs Trafford' is a more polite and formal thing to call someone, which shows that speaker B has more power in the conversation than speaker A.

A: that's fine Mrs T. (.) see what I can do for you (2) you off out tonight then (1) are you

Speaker A skips the first word of sentences — this could be part of her idiolect.

B: // yes (.) my husband's taking me to that (.) you know that new Italian restaurant in town

A: oooh (1) better get you glammed up then hadn't we (.)

B: yes (.) I must admit I did buy a new (.) oh what's it called (1) gosh how silly (1) you know (.) a (.) a dooberry haha (.) goes round your neck

Slang word, maybe part of the speaker's idiolect.

A: a (.) like a (.) scarf you mean

B: // no a (1) well sort of (.) yes (1) a (1) a (.) pashmina that's it (1) gosh I'm losing my marbles today Sandra

Speaker B's idiolect contains lots of expressions of surprise — 'gosh', 'crikey' etc.

Practice Example

Have a go at the <u>questions</u> that go with this extract and see how you get on.

1) Does speaker A use Standard or non-standard English?

2) Is this standard or non-standard grammar?

5) What does the difference in what the speakers call each other tell you about the relationship between them?

A: Lynch (1) Woodley (1) take a seat (.) I think you know why er (.) why Miss Turnbull sent you to me (3) well

B: yes (.) yes sir

C: // yeah

A: yes sir (.) Lynch (.) not yeah

C: // yes (.) sir

A: can you explain your (.) your actions

C: it were a joke (1) sir (.) we never thought she'd like start up like (.) like blubbing

A: it (.) was (.) a (.) joke (1) a joke (1) perhaps you'd find it (1) amusing if I locked you in a store cupboard (.) eh Lynch (3) answer me boy

C: // not really (.) sir

A: no (.) I rather thought not (1) and you Woodley (.) I'd thought better of you (.) anything you'd like to add

3) What's this an example of?

4) Is this
a) jargon
b) slang?

6) Write a mini-essay where you analyse the language features in this extract.
You don't just have to focus on the features that have been highlighted in the blue boxes.

Candice was never quite the same again after the store cupboard incident.

Practice Example

Finally, it's the end of the <u>mammoth</u> Section Two. Strap yourself in for the last lot of <u>questions</u>...

1) How can you tell that this is an interview?
a) the speakers take turns to speak.
b) the speakers use lots of slang.

A: now then er (1) Zoe (.) what experience have you had of working in a restaurant

2) Is this standard or non-standard English?

B: well I (.) um (.) I worked down (.) down Burgerville Saturdays

A: // yes (1) well I

B: // when I were (.) sorry (.) when I were at school

A: I er (.) wouldn't quite class Burgerville as a restaurant Zoe (2) what about silver service

3) Is this:
a) jargon
b) slang?

B: well (.) I um I done some waitressing last year in a café

A: we might be able to use you in the kitchen (1) have you had er much much experience with preparing food

4) What's this?

B: me ma hates cooking so I get the tea most nights (1) I done some right swanky stuff

5) What is this word an example of?

6) Is this
a) jargon
b) a filler?

A: the er (.) the kitchen can get very busy (.) how well do you (.) would you say you cope under pressure

7) Is this:
a) regional dialect
b) social dialect?

B: all right (.) yeah (.) I mean I (.) I do get sorta (.) mithered a bit when I don't know how to (.) how to do summat

8) Write a mini-essay where you analyse the language features in this extract. You don't just have to focus on the features that have been highlighted in the blue boxes.

Public Talk

People use language differently in speeches or presentations to how they chat with their friends.

Public Talk is usually quite Formal

1) Public speakers avoid using slang so the audience takes them seriously.
2) Speakers prepare what they're going to say to avoid stumbling or unplanned pauses.
3) They don't usually expect the audience to interact (respond) like you would in a conversation.

How you say things can Change the Meaning

There are bits of spoken language that aren't words — these help speakers connect with the audience:

1) Pauses — Pauses can be used for effect, and to help give the speech structure.
2) Tone — Tone of voice can show how a person feels, e.g. angry, sarcastic.
3) Stress — Emphasising certain words will make them stand out.
4) Rhythm — Things like three part lists and repetition can give speeches rhythm.
5) Gestures — You can make a point more forceful by doing things like banging your fist.
6) Eye contact — Speakers try to connect with their audience by looking at them directly.
7) Volume — Speakers with loud voices can seem more confident, excited or angry.

Public talk is written to Suit the Audience

1) For example, in a talk at a primary school, a speaker would use lots of eye contact and hand gestures. They might use things like alliteration, speak slowly and put lots of emphasis on descriptive words — e.g. 'the biiiiiiiiiiiiiiiig balloon burst with a big BANG!'

2) You wouldn't expect speech like this for an adult audience, e.g in a political debate.

I've got hair in strange new places — wait, that's pubic talk...

Websites like YouTube or BBC iPlayer contain loads of examples of public speaking. Listen to a few and pick out what the speakers say and do to make their speeches so incredibly gripping.

Public Talk — Worked Example

That's all very well, I hear you cry, but what does it all mean... Never fear, my eager young friend. Here's a lovely <u>worked example</u> of a written down <u>public speech</u> (rather than a transcript of one).

The speech is formal.

Eye contact — so the speaker can connect with the audience.

> Colleagues, trusted advisers, (pause, look up) *friends*.
>
> I stand before you today as a humble man. Humbled by the great honour bestowed upon me as leader of this proud party. Humbled by the confidence in me you have shown throughout this most challenging of campaigns. Humbled by the great moral duty you have entrusted me with as the new Prime Minister of this our beloved country. (Pause)
>
> And yes (nod), I also stand before you today as a proud man. Proud to be of service to my party. Proud to be of service to my community. Proud to be of service to my country.
>
> And to do that well, I need your help. Without you, I am nothing. Without you, the party is nothing. Without you, *this country* is nothing. (Pause)
>
> We must work together. There are storms ahead. Dark days in store. The road to prosperity will not be a smooth one. But we are strong. This is why the people have put their trust in us. They know that no matter what trials and tribulations lie ahead, we can deliver. And that's what we have promised. *DELIVERANCE*. (Pause)
>
> But deliverance from what?
>
> Deliverance from *poverty*, from *uncertainty* and most of all from *fear*.
>
> We are a party of promise – but not empty promises, my friends. No, no. We are a party that promises to deliver and yes, colleagues, friends, *deliver we shall*!

Gesture used to stress what he's saying.

Pause slows down the pace.

Repetition.

This speech is very rhythmic, with lots of repetition.

This word is louder to emphasise it.

Three-part list adds rhythm.

The speaker stresses these words so they stand out.

Public Talk — Practice Questions

Righty-ho. Here's a chance to see if you've been taking in any of the information on the last couple of pages — or if you've just been gazing at the page and daydreaming about your tea...

Q1   Why might public speakers avoid using slang? Choose one answer.

a) so the audience takes them seriously.

b) because slang is offensive.

c) because only teenagers use slang.

Q2   Suggest two different tones of voice you could use to change the meaning of what you say.

Q3   Suggest one hand gesture that might help a speaker to emphasise their point.

Joel got into serious trouble when he suggested the hand gesture you're all thinking of now. Tsk.

Q4   Why do public speakers try and make eye contact with the audience?

a) to show them who's in charge.

b) to try and connect with them.

c) to stop them from stumbling.

Q5   Outline two things that a speaker might do to make their speech suitable for children.

Public Talk — Practice Example

There, that wasn't too painful was it... Now have a read of this transcript of a <u>speech</u> given in a <u>school assembly</u>, and then see how you get on with the <u>questions</u>.

1) Is this formal or informal?

good morning pupils of Haverstone High School (1) teachers (.) Headmistress (1) thank you so much for inviting me here today to tell you about the charity I represent (.) Right On (1)

as some of you might already know (.) Right On is a charity that promotes the rights of children (1)

so what are children's rights (1) here are just a few (2) the right to feel safe and secure (2) the right to go to school (2) the right to health care (2)

2) Is this:
a) repetition or
b) false starts?

3) Why are there lots of pauses?

in some countries (.) there are children who work from dawn to dusk (1) some in fields (1) some in factories (1) some down mines (1) some of these children are as young as five years old (1) they have no time for play (.) no time for school (.) no time for sleep (1) the work they do affects their health (1) some of them die (3)

4) How does this affect the pace of the speech?

how does this happen (2) it happens because some people are greedy (1) they pay low wages so that they can make bigger profits (.) even if it means that children are abused and exploited (2)

5) How do you think the speaker might say these words?

Right On seeks to put an end to these practices by promoting children's rights (1) we do this through advertising (.) through publicity campaigns and by talking to people (1)

if you would like to find out more (.) please ask your teacher for one of our leaflets (1) in there you will find information about different ways you can make a difference (2) thank you for listening

6) How does the speaker connect with the audience here?

7) Write a mini-essay where you analyse the language features in this extract. You don't just have to focus on the features that have been highlighted in the blue boxes.

TV and Radio

TV and radio are both riddled with spoken language. Read on please...

There are Different Types of Spoken Language in the Media

1) Things like news reports are planned beforehand to make sure they make sense.
2) The presenters on these programmes use Standard English.
3) Language in the media can also be spontaneous (unplanned) — e.g. talk on reality shows.

Scripted speech can be written to sound Natural

1) Radio plays and TV soaps and dramas try to sound like real-life talk.
2) The actors often have regional accents and the script includes things like interruption to make it seem more realistic.
3) Scripted speech is never exactly like real-life talk. If it was then it wouldn't flow, and the audience might miss bits because people were talking at the same time. Here's an example from a TV soap opera script:

> Speakers take turns — they don't talk over each other.

> Vicky: Hey! (*she pauses*) What's your beef?
> Saul: What's it to you, eh? It's not like you gave a damn before.
> Vicky: That ain't true. (*softly*) Look, babe, it's only cos I wanna help.

> Slang is used to make the speech sound natural.

> Words are slurred together like in real-life talk.

Radio Language is Different from TV Language

1) TV language has pictures, gestures and facial expressions to help get the meaning across.
2) On the radio, everything has to be explained using words.
3) Radio presenters have to fill all the silences, so they don't pause very much.

Actually, Mum, it's for my English project...

This isn't just an opportunity to sit in front of the telly with a clipboard. You've actually got to think really carefully about the spoken language used (make sure you explain this bit to your parents).

TV and Radio — Worked Example

Make sure you've got all that in your noggin by having a read of this <u>worked example</u>
— it's a transcript of a TV news report.

The speech flows well and there are no fillers ('ums' and 'ers').

Standard English — no regional dialect or slang words.

A: good evening and welcome to the six o'clock news (.) I'm Amita Dhimar (1) tonight's headlines (1) kidnapped property developer released unharmed (2) health fears over new celebrity detox (2) petrol prices set to rise to unprecedented levels (2) tonight's top story (.) Peter Wilkinson (.) the forty-two year old multimillionaire property developer (.) kidnapped three days ago (.) has been released unharmed (1) Mr Wilkinson was seized at gunpoint on Friday evening as he returned from a night out with his wife (1) David Willets reports

Headlines use short sentences with long pauses in between as pictures are displayed.

Long sentences are used for the main report.

Lots of pauses to make sure that long sentences make sense.

B: Mr Wilkinson was found earlier today (.) in this underground car park in Bexton (1) he was bound and gagged (.) but otherwise unharmed (1) why he was taken (.) and whether a ransom had been paid for his safe return (.) is still uncertain (1) police are continuing with their investigations (1) this is David Willets (.) in Bexton (.) for Planet News (1) back to Amita in the studio

Linking phrases are used to structure the report and make it clear that this is a different story.

A: thanks David (1) in other news (1) a new detox diet (.) endorsed by celebrities including singer Mina Hurst and model Letitia Barden (.) has been criticised by health experts as barbaric and dangerous

TV and Radio — Practice Questions

Have a crack at these <u>practice questions</u> — painstakingly crafted by a team of experts to test your knowledge, intelligence and endurance, and push your performance to the limit. There, I tried to make it sound exciting — but whether you fell for it or not — you should probably <u>just do them</u>.

Q1 Is Standard English more likely to be used for:

a) a news report or

b) a soap opera?

Q2 Describe two ways that scripted speech can be made to sound natural.

Q3 Why do radio presenters try not to pause for too long?

Q4 Read these extracts from a live commentary of a football match.
Draw lines to show which one was broadcast on TV and which on the radio.

TV

> here's Saha making space along the left hand side (.)
> Cowley's in support to his right (.) cross hit hard and
> low (.) Robinson picks it up on the far right side by the
> corner flag (.) cuts inside (.) passes to Burton

Radio

> and it's Cowley (2) passes to Robinson (3)
> Robinson shoots (1) he scores

TV and Radio — Practice Example

What's even better than listening to top radio DJs yappering on? Reading them yapper on and <u>answering questions</u> on what they say... So here's a whole page for you to get stuck in to. Enjoy.

DJ Larry Longton.
What a guy.

1) Is this:
a) a filler
b) a dialect feature?

2) Is this:
a) alliteration
b) a rhetorical question?

3) Which two words have been slurred together here?

4) Why are all the pauses in this transcript so short?

5) Why does the presenter address the audience as 'my friends'?

6) Is this standard or non-standard grammar?

so (.) here we go (.) it's erm five past nine and you're listening to Radio Lynx FM (1) my name's Larry Longton (.) and I'll be taking you all the way through to twelve o clock midday (.) playing you the very best hits around (1) but first the weather (1) well (.) erm (.) guess what (.) it's gonna be cold and rainy (1) nothing new there folks (1) after all (.) it is summer (1) now a few words of wisdom for you (1) he who drinks from the sea of lurve will never be thirsty (1) I like that (1) lurve (.) lurve (.) lurve (.) OK (.) enough frivolity (.) let's get serious for a moment (1) later in the programme I'll be joined by er Holly Crowland (.) Holly is president of Youth Against Ageism (.) an organisation that seeks to seeks to challenge all forms of discrimination based on age (1) you know (.) we think that ageism only relates to older people (.) but it can be directed against younger people too (1) you can get married (.) with your parent's consent (.) at sixteen but you can't vote (1) is this right my friends (.) the minimum pay for sixteen and seventeen year olds is set lower (.) than it is for eighteens and over (.) is this fair (2) it don't don't seem very fair to me

7) Write a mini-essay where you analyse the language features in this extract.
You don't just have to focus on the features that have been highlighted in the blue boxes.

Modes

In the good old days, language was either <u>written</u> or <u>spoken</u>... sadly for you, we live in a time where there's a weird <u>mixed</u> type of language that you have to learn about — <u>multi-modal talk</u>.

Written **Language relies on** Words **to get the** Meaning **across**

1) When things are in the <u>written mode</u> (that just means they're <u>written down</u>), you <u>can't</u> see or hear things like facial expressions or tone of voice. This means that the <u>words</u> have to make the <u>meaning</u> clear.

2) Writers might try to get across things like <u>stress</u> and <u>tone</u> by using:

> • <u>underlining</u>   • CAPITALISATION
> • *italics*   • punctuation....!!??!

This is called <u>sound representation</u> — you <u>write</u> things how they might <u>sound</u> if you said them.

Spoken Language **isn't just about Words...**

1) As well as <u>what</u> speakers say, the <u>way</u> they say it is really <u>important</u>.

2) Speakers use things like <u>stress</u>, <u>volume</u> and <u>tone of voice</u> to help get their point across (see p.4).

3) Informal speech contains things like <u>self-correction</u>, <u>pauses</u>, <u>repetition</u> and <u>fillers</u> ('er', 'I mean').

Multi-Modal Talk **has Features of Speech AND Writing**

1) <u>Multi-modal</u> talk works like a <u>written down</u> version of <u>spoken</u> conversation — e.g. <u>online chat</u>.

2) This means it contains some <u>spoken language features</u>. For example:

> • <u>Small talk</u> phrases like 'hi' and 'bye'.
> • Words <u>spelt</u> the way they <u>sound</u>, e.g. 'u wanna go out 2nite?'.
> • Using <u>emoticons</u> to help get the <u>tone</u> across ☺.

Multi-modal? I prefer America's Next Top Modal...

It seems like a lot to take in, but a lot of this stuff you'll know all about from experience anyway — it's just a case of learning some fancy terms for things you do every day.

Worked Example and Practice Questions

Since you ask so nicely, I'm going to give you an example of an <u>informal email</u> between friends. And because I like you, I'll even point out some of the <u>features</u> from the previous page. Once you've had a good look at that, have a go at the <u>questions</u> to make sure you've taken everything in.

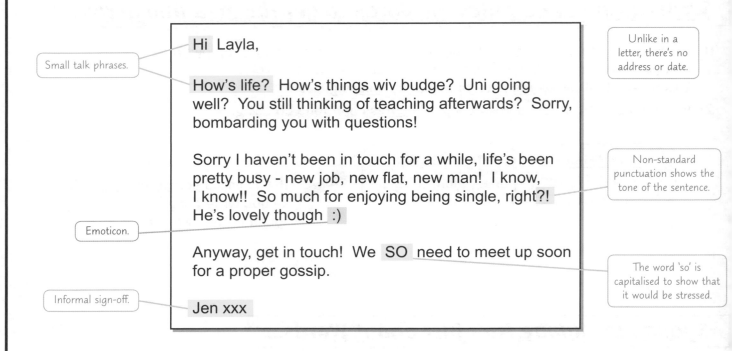

Small talk phrases.

Hi Layla,

How's life? How's things wiv budge? Uni going well? You still thinking of teaching afterwards? Sorry, bombarding you with questions!

Sorry I haven't been in touch for a while, life's been pretty busy - new job, new flat, new man! I know, I know!! So much for enjoying being single, right?! He's lovely though :)

Anyway, get in touch! We SO need to meet up soon for a proper gossip.

Jen xxx

Emoticon.

Informal sign-off.

Unlike in a letter, there's no address or date.

Non-standard punctuation shows the tone of the sentence.

The word 'so' is capitalised to show that it would be stressed.

Q1 Give two ways that you could show that a written word is stressed.

Q2 What's the correct term for phrases like 'hi' and 'how are you?'?

Q3 What is multi-modal talk? Choose one answer.

a) written language that contains elements of spoken language

b) spoken language that contains elements of written language

c) using words from different languages in the same sentence

Q4 Give two examples of types of writing that might contain multi-modal talk.

Texting

Beep-beep. Beep-beep...

Text Messages are Multi-Modal

1) Text messages contain features of <u>written language</u>.

2) They also contain features of <u>spoken language</u>
   — things like saying '<u>hi</u>' and '<u>goodbye</u>'.

3) The <u>type</u> of language in a text message can <u>vary</u>
   — e.g. a text from your network provider would
   be more formal than one from a friend.

However many times it was
explained to him, Brian never
really got the hang of texting.

Text Speak is Non-Standard

1) Words are often <u>shortened</u> in <u>text speak</u> — letters are missed out or replaced with <u>numbers</u>
   or <u>symbols</u>. This is <u>quicker</u> and <u>cheaper</u> than typing words out in full.

2) Text speak has a few rules — e.g. you normally miss out <u>vowels</u> not consonants.

3) People have their <u>own styles</u> of texting. Some people shorten every word, others write quite
   <u>formally</u>. Most people are quite <u>inconsistent</u>, but text speak still has some <u>common features</u>:

FEATURE	EXAMPLE
Numbers and symbols instead of words	4 (for), & (and)
Shortening words, missing out vowels	jan (January), wk (week)
Writing words the way they sound	c u (see you)
Acronyms* (just writing the first letter of each word)	rofl (Rolling On Floor Laughing)
Initialisms* (just writing the first letter of each word)	brb (Be Right Back)
Smileys / emoticons	;-) (wink)
Words missed out and simple sentences	be back soon
Non-standard grammar, punctuation and no capitals	im not bad hows u

*Watch out — it's easy to get <u>confused</u> between acronyms and initialisms. For <u>acronyms</u> the <u>whole
new word</u> can be pronounced (e.g. ASBO) but for <u>initialisms</u> each letter is said <u>separately</u> (e.g. DNA).

Let's talk about texts, baby...

Texting might be a piece of cake for you young whippersnappers, but not everyone finds it so easy.
My poor old mum doesn't know how to do punctuation, so she sends me texts like this — 'hello
darling comma how are you question mark'. And my dad's fingers are too big for the buttons. Bless.

Texting

Text messages are a <u>fast</u> and <u>casual</u> form of communication. People like them because you can send one <u>quickly</u>, and <u>reply</u> to one whenever you want to (or just pretend you didn't get it...).

Text Language *has its own Rules*

1) Writing a message in <u>capitals</u> makes it look like you're <u>shouting</u>, so people do it to <u>emphasise</u> words — e.g. 'WOOHOO'.

2) This is <u>sound representation</u> (see p.35).

3) It's tricky to get across the <u>tone</u> you want in not many words.

4) So, to make sure you don't <u>offend</u> someone, you might put something like a winking face to show you're joking.

Mark <u>really</u> wished he'd remembered to use a winking face when he called the Flint brothers 'sissy nancy boys'.

Text Speak *is Changing over Time*

1) A few years ago, mobiles <u>couldn't</u> do <u>predictive text</u>, and sending texts was more <u>expensive</u> than it is now. So by using text speak people could <u>save time</u> and <u>money</u>.

2) Now phones have got predictive text, it's often <u>quicker</u> and <u>easier</u> to type words out <u>in full</u>. So text speak might be used <u>less</u> than it was a few years ago.

3) Words also go in and out of <u>fashion</u> really quickly — e.g. <u>lol</u> used to stand for '<u>lots of love</u>', but most people these days use it to mean '<u>laugh out loud</u>'.

Some people think *Text Speak is 'Bad' English*

1) Text speak uses <u>non-standard English</u>, so some people think it's '<u>incorrect</u>' and means people will stop being able to <u>spell</u> words properly.

2) Other people say that text speak is <u>useful</u> for text messages, but that it <u>shouldn't</u> be used in other writing, e.g. in your homework or exams.

3) You could also argue that language is always <u>changing</u>, and text speak is the <u>next step</u>.

2 txt or nt 2 txt... thts the qstn

Some people think that texting will lead to a generation of people who can't spell. But who decided the 'correct' way to spell anyway... Oo I've come over all anti-establishment. Time for a lie down.

Texting — Worked Example

I've got loads of friends, so I get hundreds of text messages a day. Here's an example of the kind of hilarious things we say to each other, with some notes on the important features of the language.

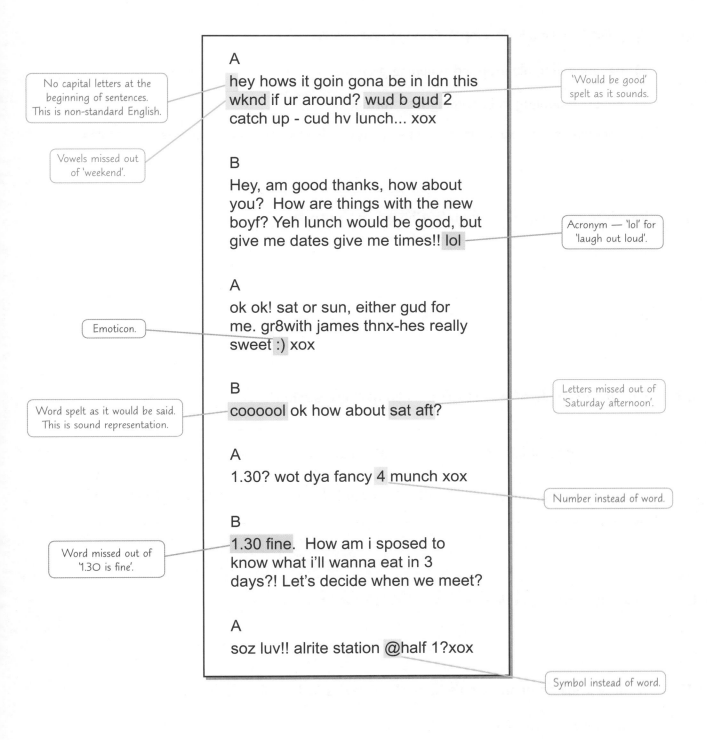

No capital letters at the beginning of sentences. This is non-standard English.

Vowels missed out of 'weekend'.

'Would be good' spelt as it sounds.

Acronym — 'lol' for 'laugh out loud'.

Emoticon.

Word spelt as it would be said. This is sound representation.

Letters missed out of 'Saturday afternoon'.

Number instead of word.

Word missed out of '1.30 is fine'.

Symbol instead of word.

A
hey hows it goin gona be in ldn this wknd if ur around? wud b gud 2 catch up - cud hv lunch... xox

B
Hey, am good thanks, how about you? How are things with the new boyf? Yeh lunch would be good, but give me dates give me times!! lol

A
ok ok! sat or sun, either gud for me. gr8with james thnx-hes really sweet :) xox

B
coooool ok how about sat aft?

A
1.30? wot dya fancy 4 munch xox

B
1.30 fine. How am i sposed to know what i'll wanna eat in 3 days?! Let's decide when we meet?

A
soz luv!! alrite station @half 1?xox

Texting — Practice Questions

Sending texts may be simple, but it's not allowed in the controlled assessment... Instead, you have to know how to <u>write about</u> them, so have a go at these <u>questions</u> to check you're on track.

Q1 Why did text speak develop? Choose one answer.

   a) because schools stopped teaching grammar

   b) because society is becoming less formal

   c) because it was easier and cheaper to type shorter versions of words on mobiles

Q2 Which of these is an acronym? Choose one answer.

   a) FIFA

   b) :o)

   c) BBC

Q3 Find the example of text speak in each of these sentences.

a) R u coming later?	c) That's gr8.	e) See you tmrw.
b) I'm @ my mum's.	d) She's my bff.	f) Out with Greg.

Q4 Why might someone add an emoticon to a text message?

Q5 What worries do some people have about text speak? Choose one answer.

   a) it might go out of fashion

   b) people won't be able to spell words properly anymore

   c) it's confusing for old people

Texting — Practice Example

More texts from another one of my <u>many friends</u>... Have a <u>read through</u> them and answer the <u>questions</u>. Use the information on pages 37-38 to help you <u>analyse</u> the <u>language</u>.

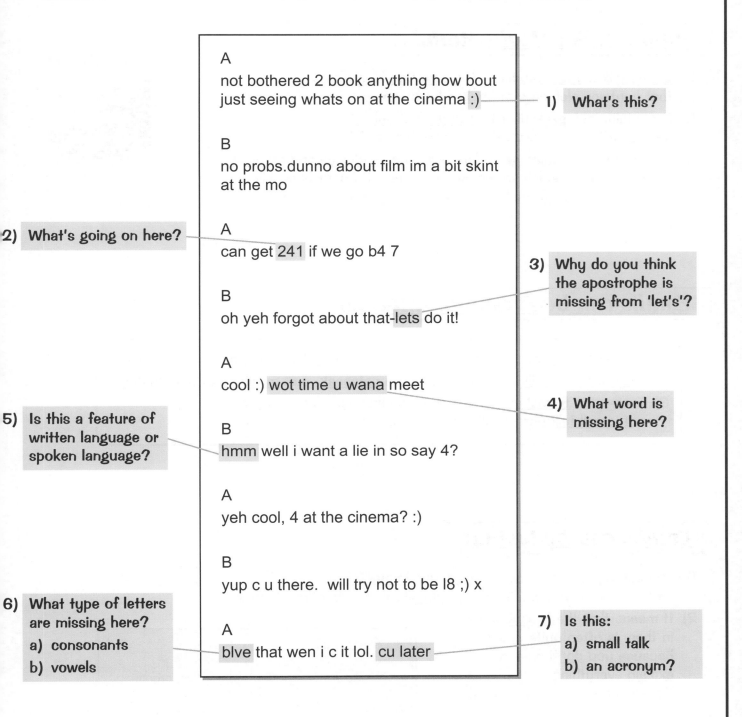

A

not bothered 2 book anything how bout just seeing whats on at the cinema :)

1) What's this?

B

no probs.dunno about film im a bit skint at the mo

2) What's going on here?

A

can get 241 if we go b4 7

3) Why do you think the apostrophe is missing from 'let's'?

B

oh yeh forgot about that-lets do it!

A

cool :) wot time u wana meet

4) What word is missing here?

5) Is this a feature of written language or spoken language?

B

hmm well i want a lie in so say 4?

A

yeh cool, 4 at the cinema? :)

B

yup c u there. will try not to be l8 ;) x

6) What type of letters are missing here?
a) consonants
b) vowels

A

blve that wen i c it lol. cu later

7) Is this:
a) small talk
b) an acronym?

8) Write a mini-essay where you analyse the language features in this extract. You don't just have to focus on the features that have been highlighted in the blue boxes.

Online Talk

The internet has changed the way that people <u>communicate</u> and the kind of <u>language</u> that they use. Some of the best examples of this are <u>emails</u>, <u>instant messaging</u>, <u>chat rooms</u> and <u>online gaming</u>.

Online Talk *is Multi-Modal*

1) <u>Online talk</u> is <u>multi-modal</u> — it's a <u>written</u> language that contains elements of <u>spoken</u> language.

2) It contains <u>netspeak</u> (like <u>text speak</u> but <u>online</u>) — e.g. letters replaced with numbers (see p.37).

3) How <u>formal</u> the language is depends on its <u>audience</u> and <u>purpose</u>. For example, an email arranging a meeting with your <u>boss</u> will probably be <u>more formal</u> than one catching up with a <u>friend</u>.

Before the internet was invented, people had to make their own entertainment.

Emails *can be* Formal *or* Informal

1) <u>Formal emails</u> (e.g. at work) usually contain <u>Standard English</u>.

2) <u>Less formal emails</u> might contain more <u>netspeak</u>, e.g. <u>missing out punctuation</u>.

3) Even quite <u>formal emails</u> use some <u>spoken language features</u>, e.g. <u>small talk</u> phrases like 'hi' and 'see you'.

Emails *can be* Instant

1) You can reply to an email pretty much <u>immediately</u>. This makes them more like <u>conversations</u> than a traditional letter.

2) It means that the <u>language</u> used in them is often quite <u>direct</u>, because you <u>don't</u> have to <u>explain</u> everything. For example: ⟶

> Hi Claire,
>
> What time are we meeting today? I've forgotten...
>
> Thanks
>
> Polly

Virtual men — e-males...

Ho hum, it's all getting a bit simple now really. If this stuff about emails is too easy, or you're just into punishment, try putting the page next to a mirror and reading it all backwards or something.

Online Talk

So we've done <u>emails</u> — they were dead easy. Now it's <u>instant message</u> time.

Instant Messages **are** Informal

1) People often use <u>non-standard English</u> in <u>instant messages</u>.
2) You're online <u>at the same time</u> as someone, so people type quickly.
   They often use <u>netspeak</u> to save time and effort.
3) How you write probably <u>changes</u> depending on <u>who</u> you're talking to, e.g. you might
   use less netspeak if you're chatting to your mum than to your mate.

You usually Take Turns *when you're* Messaging

People often show whose <u>turn</u> it is by asking a <u>question</u>
at the <u>end</u> of each message, for example:

Jim:	How u doin?
Saz:	gud thnx, u?
Jim:	yeh not bad,you out later?

Ed: u typin wiv ur feet again?
Hayley: yeh it rox!! u never tried it?
Ed: nah. hands 4 me evry time
Hayley: lol

Keeping someone <u>waiting</u> for a long time before you reply could be
seen as <u>rude</u>, so people use <u>initialisms</u> like 'BRB' ('be right back') or
'GTG' ('got to go') to show that they'll be <u>out of touch</u> for a while.

People use Sound Representation

1) You can show things like tone of voice using <u>sound representation</u> (see p. 35).
2) For example, you might write 'NOOOOOO waaaaaaaaay!?!' to make it clear that if
   you were speaking out loud you'd be shouting, and would sound really surprised.
3) You can show facial expressions using <u>emoticons</u> ☺.

Learn all this and you'll be ROFLing...
Call me a miserable old git, but I can't remember a single time when I've found something so
amusing that I've actually rolled on the floor laughing. Although I did once burst with laughter.

Online Talk

Personally I'm not keen on the word <u>blog</u>. It kind of reminds me of throwing up. Still, you don't have to like it, you just have to read it. And maybe it doesn't even remind you of sick anyway, who knows...

Blogs are like Public Diaries

1) <u>Blogs</u> let people share their thoughts with the rest of the world.
2) <u>Blog writers</u> don't necessarily <u>interact</u> with the people reading their blog, but some readers might <u>post</u> comments on the blog after they've read it.
3) Some blog writers use <u>Standard English</u>. Others use <u>netspeak</u>.

> <u>Social networking sites</u> like Facebook® and Twitter act like <u>microblogs</u> — people record what they're doing during the day. The language is really <u>varied</u>.

Different Types of Websites use Different Language

1) In <u>chat rooms</u> and <u>forums</u> you talk to <u>everyone</u> else who's on the same site.
2) They're often based on <u>hobbies</u> or <u>interests</u>, so they contain <u>jargon</u> words about specific topics.
3) Chat room conversations are <u>quick</u>, so <u>netspeak</u> is often used to <u>save time</u>.

The Internet has had a big Impact on English

- The internet has changed English — there are lots of <u>new words</u> about it, like 'website' and 'search engine'.
- It's also changing the way that people <u>speak</u>, e.g. some people might say 'lol' in a spoken conversation now.
- This is particularly true of <u>young people</u>, and shows how <u>technology</u> is <u>changing</u> the language.

Sandra was delighted with her web site — face-height, right across the footpath.

Check out my blog — 1412 entries about my cats...

...and 1246 entries about my lack of a boyfriend. I just don't understand it, I mean, I'm interesting and funny, plus I've got a huge collection of stuffed toys. Any man would be lucky to have me.

Online Talk — Worked Example

You need to be able to recognise different <u>features</u> of online talk when you see them.
Here's an <u>example</u> of an instant messenger conversation that I've helpfully marked up for you.

A: hey sweetie, hows u?

B: gud thanx, u?

A: ok. am @ emmas doin history coursework ☹

B: ugh havent started mine. u & em r sooooo lucky u got put togeva, i got put wiv freaky ian

A: lol. least hes brainy, u'll get an A for sure ☺

B: yeahhh but... i wanna be wiv u guys!!!

A: i no!!! sooooo wish we cud all do it togevr. oooh, hannah's just come on - ttyl

B: ok.

B: u there?

A: soz hun, jus seein if han's ok. u no she split wiv Harry?

B: OMG. wen?

A: afta skool 2day. he dumped her in front of evry1...

B: OMG. poor han. is she ok?

A: not gr8. shes comin ova now. u wanna cum ova 2?

No capital letters at the beginning of sentences. This is non-standard English.

Symbol instead of 'at'.

Emoticon.

Poor freaky Ian just didn't know where he was going wrong.

Spelling shows how you would say the word.

Non-standard punctuation — extra exclamation marks show the tone of the sentence.

Initialism — 'ttyl' for 'talk to you later'.

Initialism — 'OMG' for 'Oh My God'.

Number instead of word. This is non-standard English.

Words slurred together shows how you might say them.

No apostrophe in 'she's'. This is non-standard punctuation.

Online Talk — Worked Example

So, spending time on Facebook® now counts as homework too. Tcchhh, it wasn't like that in my day. Tear yourself away from your computer and have a gander at this worked example from a chat room.

Small talk that you'd normally use in speech.

A: hey guys. me & the missus r off to the Dales nxt wknd. any tips for good (non-tourist!) climbs?

Capital letters make it look like speaker is shouting.

B: Nice one m8, dales are awsum! Try Gilberts Edge nr brantmoor — QUALITY!!!

Jargon.

No capital letters or punctuation. This is non-standard English.

A: cheers mate forgot to say we're both about a grade 5

C: Gilbert's Edge is a great route. It gets pretty busy though... My top tip — Willet Tor, near Fenstone.

Netspeak — vowels missed out.

D: Dales!! ace!! me & mine used to cruz rnd lookin 4 gud boulderin spots. bst we found was glassley heights — jsut off the B648 nr stoke worthy

Typing quickly means that typos are common.

A: great, ta guys. should give us summat to work with :o)

Regional dialect word.

E: hey hey. soz to crash this thread lol. just wondrd if ne1 cud recommend sum gud shoes — thinkin of gettin the new Rockgod Scramblers — ne1 tried em?

C: No worries. A friend of mine just got a pair and swears by them. They're on offer at the mo at SportsWorld — I've got a discount code if you're interested.

Missing letters.

Numbers used instead of words.

E: nice 1 m8 ur a proper gent

Word spelt as it would be said.

C: Er... thank you... I'm actually a laydeee, but the light's quite dim in here ;)

E: oh heck, soz luv. im sure ur gorgeous ;) lol

Acronym.

C: Thank you, I am.

Online Talk — Practice Questions

Nobody panic, I haven't forgotten the <u>practice questions</u>, I just got a bit carried away with examples. Here they are, knock yourself out. I'm off for a little lie down to get over all the excitement.

Q1 Give an example of a small talk phrase that might be used in an email.

Q2 For each of the following language features, put a tick in the box to suggest whether they would be used in a formal business email, an instant messenger conversation, or both.

Feature	Formal email	Instant message
Missing punctuation		
Small talk phrases		
Standard English		
Emoticons		

Q3 How might you show whose turn it is to type when you're instant messaging someone?

"He still hasn't replied."
"Maybe you shouldn't have sent the picture of yourself."

Q4 How might you write a word if you want it to look like you're shouting?

Q5 How has the internet changed the English language? Choose one answer.

a) it has led to lots of new words

b) people don't talk to each other any more

c) it hasn't changed the language

Online Talk — Practice Example

Pssst, yeah you, over here... I've got a lovely <u>example</u> of an <u>instant messenger</u> conversation here. It's going cheap. Look, I tell you what, because I like the look of you I'm going to let you have it for nothing. Just don't tell anyone, or my rep will be in tatters...

1) Is this:
a) a filler
b) small talk?

3) Is this a feature of written language or spoken language?

6) What punctuation is missing here?

A: alrite m8, wot u doin?

B: Revisin. Got me drivin test 2moz am. Told ya lst wk

A: Oops my bad. Gd luk. u scared?

B: Kinda. had 2 lsns 2 day. Only hit kerb once ;o)

A: ur dangerous man - aint never gonna get in the car wiv you lol

B: Oh yeah. Once I got wheels yule be beggin

A: Y wd I wanna commit suicide? Im 2 young 2 die :)

B: NEway don't worry I aint gonna pass.

A: That's gud man. Think how many lives ur savin.

B: LMAO... not. Wot u up to 2nite?

---

2) Why are letters missed out like this?

4) Is this an:
a) initialism
b) acronym?

5) What's this?

7) Why do you think a lot of posts end with a question?

8) Write a mini-essay where you analyse the language features in this extract. You don't just have to focus on the features that have been highlighted in the blue boxes.

Online Talk — Practice Example

Well, this is it. Your last <u>practice example</u>. I know it's terribly sad, but don't worry, all the unused practice examples have been sent off to a big factory to get recycled into plastic bags. Apart from the bad ones. They're going to be made into scratching posts for cows. Anyway, this blog is one of the lucky ones that made the cut. Read and enjoy.

One man's crusade against bad English
by Gerald Pearson

As my regular readers will know, I'm fighting an ongoing battle to prevent the tragic decline of language skills in today's youth. This week heralds a new personal low; on Monday I saw Gideon 'instant messaging' a friend the following tripe: 'OMG - aged p jus trpd ova my sktbrd & i got it on flm. utube gold. ROFLMAO!!!' I'm unable to interpret what on earth he's talking about, but naturally I withdrew his internet rights immediately. I've told him he cna have them back once he's finished reading War and Peace.

I can only be grateful that we removed Felicity to finishing school in Switzerland after the text messaging fiasco. At least she's out of temptation's way.

My crusade hit another stumbling block this week, when I received a letter from Gideon's school regarding changes to the syllabus. It seems that 'text speak' is to be taught as part of the English Language GCSE!?! A dreadful setback, dear readers, but I shall not yield!

Ah, dearest wife is calling, I must away. Goodbye all.

---

1) What's this?

2) What's going on here?

3) What's going on here?

4) Is this punctuation standard or non-standard?

5) Is this a feature of written language or spoken language?

6) What's this an example of?

7) Write a mini-essay where you analyse the language features in this extract. You don't just have to focus on the features that have been highlighted in the blue boxes.

What You Have to Do

For <u>Unit 3</u> <u>Part C</u> (Spoken Language Study) you have to do a <u>Controlled Assessment Task</u>. This is worth <u>10%</u> of the total mark for your GCSE. It doesn't sound like much but it's marks in the bag.

There's a Choice of Six Tasks

1) You or your teacher will have to choose <u>one task</u> out of <u>six</u> for you to answer.

2) The task will ask you to <u>analyse</u> some spoken language <u>data</u> in one of the following categories:

- Social attitudes to spoken language
  — e.g. your <u>own language</u> and other people's <u>attitudes</u> to it.
- Spoken genres — e.g. the language of a <u>speech</u> or a <u>TV interview</u>.
- Multi-modal talk — e.g. some <u>text messages</u>.

There'll be two tasks for each of these categories.

The Controlled Assessment is Timed

1) You write your answer under <u>supervised conditions</u>.
   It's like a <u>cross</u> between <u>coursework</u> and an <u>exam</u>.

2) You'll have up to <u>three hours</u> to write <u>800-1000 words</u>.

3) The time might be <u>spread over</u> two or more sessions.

You can Prepare for your Controlled Assessment

While you're <u>planning your answer</u>, you can:

- <u>Work in small groups</u>.
- Get help from your <u>teacher</u>.

Any work you do during the <u>supervised sessions</u> needs to be <u>handed in</u> to your teacher at the end. You'll <u>get it back</u> at the start of the next session.

During the <u>assessment</u>:

- You can take <u>brief notes from your plan</u> in with you, but <u>NOT drafts</u>.
- You'll get <u>2-3 hours</u> to write up your work.
- Your final piece can be <u>handwritten</u> or <u>written on the computer</u>.

A cordless melon's tents* — not so scary from that angle...

Not the most fascinating page, I'm sure you'll agree, but it helps to know exactly what you're going to have to do, and how long you're going to have to do it, and how many words you're going to...

*Yes, that is an anagram of 'controlled assessment'.

How to Analyse Data

So, you've got a lovely <u>transcript</u> but no idea how to <u>analyse</u> it. That's where this page comes in...

Your <u>Data</u> _is the spoken language you'll be_ <u>Analysing</u>

There are all sorts of different <u>types</u> of <u>data</u> that you could look at for your controlled assessment. For example:

1) <u>Transcripts</u> of <u>real-life talk</u>.
2) <u>Transcripts of audio</u> clips (e.g. a radio show or a TV interview).
3) <u>Text messages</u> or <u>online chat</u> conversations.
4) <u>Scripted language</u> (e.g. a radio advert or public speech).
5) Newspaper <u>articles</u>, or other material that shows people's <u>attitudes</u> to <u>spoken</u> language.

Write Down _the_ Basic Information _first_

Make sure you <u>jot down</u> the really <u>obvious</u> things that you'll consider in your analysis. For example:

1) What <u>kind</u> of <u>spoken language</u> it is, e.g. a <u>conversation</u>, a <u>speech</u> or an <u>interview</u>.
2) The speakers' background — e.g. their <u>age</u>, <u>gender</u>, <u>job</u> and <u>social background</u>.
3) The <u>topic</u> — e.g. if they're talking about cars, there'll be <u>jargon</u> words to look out for.
4) The <u>context</u> — e.g. if it's a <u>job interview</u>, you might expect <u>formal</u> speech and <u>jargon</u>.

Get Stuck In _and Start Analysing_ the Actual Language

1) Look out for <u>non-fluency</u> features like <u>pauses</u>, <u>fillers</u>, <u>false starts</u> and <u>repetition</u> (see p. 4).
2) Listen out for <u>accents</u> and changes in <u>tone of voice</u> and <u>volume</u>.
3) Mention any examples of non-standard <u>grammar</u> (e.g. 'We was trying our hardest').
4) The way the speakers <u>interact</u> is important too — e.g. who speaks most and what they call each other.
5) If you're looking at <u>multi-modal talk</u>, you could look at how things like <u>emoticons</u> are used.

28 Days' Data — now that would be scary...
It's really helpful to think about the speakers and the topic they're discussing before you start analysing the language. That way you can think about which language features to look out for.

How to Write Up the Controlled Assessment

The previous page gave you an idea of the <u>kind of things</u> you need to write about.
This page'll tell you how to write a <u>really great</u> analysis.

Think about *How you'll Structure your Work*

A <u>three-part</u> structure is best:

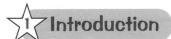  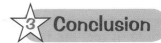

When you give in your <u>final draft</u>, make sure you also hand in your <u>data</u> and <u>notes</u>.

Make Sure *you have a Good Introduction*

In your introduction you need to say something about:

* what <u>kind of spoken language</u> you're looking at.
* what <u>features</u> of it you're going to discuss.
* where the <u>data</u> is <u>from</u> — e.g. 'this is a TV interview'.

The *Data Analysis* should be the *Main Bit of your Answer*

Use <u>paragraphs</u> to <u>structure</u> your answer. For example, you might have paragraphs about:

* Vocabulary (e.g. slang, jargon, dialect words)
* Accent/dialect
* Grammar (e.g. standard or non-standard)
* Non-fluency features (e.g. pauses, false starts, interruption)
* Elements of spoken language that aren't words (e.g. loudness, stress, tone of voice)

Finish *with a Conclusion*

1) In your <u>last paragraph</u>, you should sum up what you've found out.
2) Remember to refer back to the <u>question</u> — say what your data
   shows and how it <u>answers</u> the question.
   3) Then you'll be as <u>happy</u> as this lady.

Blah blah pun — something something joke...

You get the idea. If you can get a good structure from the start, your answer should fall
effortlessly into place. The controlled assessment can be a gold mine of marks if you plan properly.

Sample Task — Social Attitudes to Spoken Language

There will be <u>two tasks</u> to choose from on <u>social attitudes to spoken language</u>.

Here's an Example of what you can Expect...

You could choose a task for your <u>controlled assessment</u> that looks a bit like the one below.

> Reflect on the speech used by young people.
> What attitudes towards it are you aware of from others?

1) Your teacher will give you the <u>data</u> or tell you where to find it.
2) It might be a good idea to find out a bit about <u>attitudes</u> to spoken language — e.g. a newspaper article about teenage slang.

...and Here's what your Data might look like

Aimee:	why don't we go to Roxy's (.) yeah Roxy's (1) last week was awesome
Mo:	yeah (.) Roxy's is good but (.) er it's so expensive babe (.) anyways (1) erm don't get paid till Saturday
Aimee:	the DJ was sick though Mo (.) er can't you borrow some dosh from Akkie
Mo:	nah (.) you know what he's like (.) mean or what
Aimee:	// well I could lend you some hun
Mo:	nah babe (1) I'm always (.) I've been cadgin off of you loads (.) it ain't fair
Aimee:	I could come round to yours then
Mo:	would you (.) hey but you don't get don't get to go out then so it's
Aimee:	// I'm not that bothered and erm (.) we can like watch a film or somethin (2) yeah an we could we could go to Dino's like get a pizza (.) or somethin
Mo:	// yeah but I'm payin babe
Aimee:	you just said you ain't got none
Mo:	I got some money (2) just just not enough to go to Roxy's

> **Key**
> (1) = pause in seconds
> (.) = micropause

1) You'll probably be looking at something a bit <u>longer</u> than this.
2) To give you an idea of what you could say about it, there's a <u>sample answer</u> on page 54.

Hands up if reading that made you want a pizza too...

Once you've got your data, you're ready to start thinking about what it all means. But before you do that, get on the phone to Dino's and celebrate the start of the controlled assessment in style. Mmm.

SECTION FIVE — THE CONTROLLED ASSESSMENT

Sample Answer — Social Attitudes to Spoken Language

In your <u>write-up</u> you need to mention the <u>relevant things</u> you've spotted in your data and what they tell you about the spoken language you're studying. Here's part of an answer to give you some ideas.

Remember *to* Focus *your answer on* Social Attitudes

Introduction

Explains what you're looking at from the start.

Social attitudes towards the way young people speak are often quite negative. For example, some people think that teenagers use too much slang, and too many 'vague' words such as 'like' and 'sort of'. They think that this is ruining the English language.

Analysis

Give examples to support each point you make.

The speakers in this extract are both in year 11 and live in Gillingham, Kent. Both speakers use Estuary English, and there are some features of this dialect in the transcript. For example, the word 'ain't' is used by both of them, e.g. Mo says 'it ain't fair'. Also, they both miss off consonants at the ends of words, for example 'cadgin', 'somethin'.

Start a new paragraph for each new point.

They use slang words, for example using 'sick' to mean 'good' and 'dosh' to mean 'money'. Slang words are often used between friends, but the speakers probably wouldn't use them if they were talking to a teacher.

Good use of technical terms.

The way they talk to each other shows that their relationship is informal and affectionate. Mo calls Aimee 'babe' three times, so the word is probably part of his idiolect. A feature of Aimee's idiolect is that she uses the word 'like' a lot, e.g. 'we can like watch a film or somethin'. This is 'vague' language. Some people think that 'vague' language makes speech hard to understand, but it's clear what Aimee means.

Remember to explain how each point relates to the question.

The conversation contains fillers ('er' and 'erm'), repetition ('just just') and false starts ('I'm always I've been cadging off of you loads'). These features are typical in most real-life conversations, because the speakers haven't planned what they are going to say, so it's not only teenagers that use them.

Conclusion

Sum up your main points and refer back to the question.

In conclusion, my data shows that when teenagers are talking to each other in an informal setting, they use slang and non-standard grammar. However, their meaning is still clear. The way teenagers talk is different to the way older people talk, so it is changing the English language, but this does not mean that it is ruining it.

In conclusion — we rock!!!

Sample Task — Spoken Genres

Just like for <u>social attitudes to spoken language</u>, you can <u>choose</u> from <u>two tasks</u> for <u>spoken genres</u>.

Here is an Example of what you can Expect...

Explore the language features of a type of talk in the media, such as a television or radio script.

1) Your teacher will give you an <u>extract</u> from some spoken language in the media to work with, or tell you where to find it.
2) Your extract is likely to be <u>longer</u> than the one below.

Not to be confused with 1981's Punk-Jazz sensations, 'Broken Genres'.

...and Here's what your Data might look like

Tim: [*blustering*] Now look here, Inspector, I don't know what the problem is here but you really can't go round accusing people like this. You have absolutely no evid-

McRae: [*interrupts sharply*] No evidence, Mr Fanshaw? I have all the evidence I need to make sure you and your *sister* won't be seeing daylight for quite some time.

Tim: [*gasps*] My-my sister? But I don't have a -

McRae: [*loudly and angrily*] Don't take me for a fool! Sergeant, bring in Miss Fanshaw. [*Turns and looks hard at Tim*] Or *Miss Brown*, as she's been calling herself lately.

Tim: [*regaining his composure*] *Miss Brown*? [*He laughs*] My cleaning lady? Why, the woman's common as muck. [*With disgust*] Certainly no relative of mine.

Enter Sergeant Reeves and Sally.

Sally: Why 'ello there, Inspector, was yer after another o' me home-made stotties?

McRae: You can drop the act, *Miss Fanshaw*. You may as well come clean, I know you have the manuscript, and what's more I can prove it.

Sally: [*a little too quickly*] Manuscript, sir? I- I'm sure I don't know nothin' about no manuscript. [*Holds her hands up in defeat*] Why, I can't even read, me.

To give you an idea of what you could say about this data, there's a <u>sample answer</u> on page 56.

Don't stop now — it's just getting interesting...

Oh no, that's the end of the extract and I've got more questions than a three-hour maths exam — just who is Sally, where's the missing manuscript, and what on earth's a stottie...

Sample Answer — Spoken Genres

The <u>sample answer</u> on this page will hopefully give you an idea of the sort of <u>features</u> to <u>pick up on</u>.

Remember to Focus your answer on Spoken Genres

Introduction

State what it is that you want to look at.

Television and radio dramas have to sound like real-life speech, but they have to be easier to follow than real-life speech, so that the audience understands them. Script-writers can make speech sound natural by using regional accents or dialects, slang, fillers and interruption. They can also tell the actors to stress words or change their volume or tone of voice. I would expect to see examples of these things in most scripts.

Analysis

Remember to mention the context of your data.

I analysed part of a script for a TV crime drama. Tim and McRae use Standard English, but Sally uses non-standard grammar and pronunciation (e.g. 'I don't know nothin' instead of 'I don't know anything' and 'yer' instead of 'you') and dialect words (e.g. 'stotties'). This shows that the character would have a regional accent and dialect.

Explaining why the script is written as it is will bag you extra marks.

McRae interrupts Tim twice, which makes the speech sound more natural. The interruptions don't stop the audience understanding the dialogue, for example McRae finishes Tim's sentence ("No evidence, Mr Fanshaw?"), so that the audience know what Tim was going to say. There are also examples of repetition ("My-my sister?") and false starts ("I- I'm").

The punctuation and stage directions show the actors when to pause. For example, the full stop and stage direction 'Turns and looks hard at Tim', suggests that there is a long pause before McRae's next line.

Give examples to back up your points.

The stage directions also show the parts of spoken language that aren't words. For example, 'loudly and angrily' shows the character's volume and tone of voice. The italics show which words should be stressed, e.g. 'your *sister*'. Things like facial expressions and hand gestures also help scripted speech sound/look more real. These are shown by stage directions like 'gasps' and 'holds her hands up in defeat'.

Include as many relevant features as you can think of.

Conclusion

Sum up your main points at the end.

The script contains regional dialect, interruption and indications of how stress, tone of voice and hand gestures should be used. These are used carefully so that they make the dialogue sound natural without making it confusing for the audience.

SECTION FIVE — THE CONTROLLED ASSESSMENT

Sample Task — Multi-Modal Talk

The last pair of tasks that you can choose from will both be on multi-modal talk.

Here is an Example of what you can Expect...

> Investigate the language of online talk. How does it relate to spoken conversations?

1) Your teacher will give you an extract from a multi-modal conversation, e.g. an online chat or a text message conversation.
2) You'll probably want to analyse a longer extract than the one below.

...and Here's what your Data might look like

This extract was taken from an instant messenger conversation between a father and son.

```
DAD:   Hi Will
WILL:  hey
DAD:   What u up to?
WILL:  workin. Got an essay 2 b in tomoz. Then I'm finishd 4 the yr :-)
DAD:   Then exams?
WILL:  No exams this yr!!!
DAD:   What a doddle! weren't like that in my day me laddie.
WILL:  :P
DAD:   Did mum tell u bout the cat? He's got cancer. in his ear.
WILL:  Serious? :-O omg
DAD:   Yep. Gotta have his ear taken off.
WILL:  ah...poor Gavin :-(
DAD:   Well...least it'll give him a few more years...anyway, going to China in August
WILL:  Cooool.  Brng us sumthin bck
DAD:   Course! Stick of rock OK?!
WILL:  lol
DAD:   Gotta go.  C u later xxx
WILL:  Byeeeeeeeee! xxx
```

Never mind chatting to your dad — get on with that essay...

To give you an idea of what you could say about this data, there's a sample answer, on page 58.

For the 100th time, Mum — it does not mean 'lots of love'...
Iv ritten a top tip 4u 2 tel u not 2 wste tym wen ur revisin 4 ur xams. lol. also if uv bin payin @tention u shud no wot im sayin an b able 2 rite bout the dffrnt features ov my lang. :D x x x

Sample Answer — Multi-Modal Talk

Have a look at the <u>sample answer below</u>. Don't just <u>read</u> it though — <u>think</u> about what you would have said if you had <u>analysed</u> the same data and how you might have <u>structured</u> your answer too.

Remember *to Focus your answer on Multi-Modal Talk*

Introduction

Show how you're going to answer the question.

Online talk is multi-modal — it's written language that contains elements of spoken language. I studied an instant messenger conversation between a father and son. I wanted to look at how the speakers used netspeak to make the conversation more like spoken language. Some people think netspeak is only used by teenagers, so I also wanted to find out whether it's used more by someone younger than someone older.

Analysis

Talk about the overall structure first, then the detail.

The conversation starts with the small talk expressions 'Hi' and 'hey', which show that the relationship between the people is informal and friendly. For the rest of the conversation the people take turns, sometimes using a question at the end of a message to show that they have finished typing, e.g. 'What u up to?'.

Use paragraphs to structure your answer.

Both people miss out letters from words (e.g. 'workin', 'yr') and spell things the way they sound (e.g. 'C u' instead of 'see you'), but Will uses them more than his dad. Will also uses a lot of acronyms and initialisms (e.g. 'lol', 'omg'), which are not used by his dad.

Talk about similarities and differences between speakers.

Both people miss out words and use simple sentences, e.g. 'going to China in August' instead of 'I'm going to China in August', and 'Serious?' rather than 'Is it serious?'. Will tends to shorten sentences more than his father.

Give examples to back up all your points.

Will uses emoticons (e.g. :-), :-O) a lot to show his facial expression, whereas his father doesn't. Both people use non-standard punctuation and spelling to show the parts of language that aren't words. For example, Will's dad says 'Stick of rock OK?!' to show that he is joking. Will writes 'Byeeeeeeeee!' to show how he would say the word if it was a spoken conversation.

Conclusion

Sum up what you've found out at the end.

Both people miss out letters, use simple sentences and non-standard spelling/ punctuation to make the 'chat' seem more like spoken language. The younger person also used acronyms and emoticons. This suggests that netspeak is used more by younger people than by older people, just like slang and non-standard English are used more by young people in spoken language.

Glossary

accent	The way that words are <u>pronounced</u> — it's affected by <u>where</u> you're from and your <u>background</u>.
dialect	A <u>way of speaking</u> that uses particular <u>vocabulary</u> and <u>grammar</u>, and sometimes has an <u>accent</u> to go with it.
discourse	The <u>set language routines</u> people use in certain situations, e.g. in a restaurant people might say things like "Would you like to see the dessert list?" and "I'd like the bill, please."
feedback	The things that people do to show that they're <u>listening</u> to the speaker and they <u>understand</u> or <u>agree</u> with what's being said — e.g. saying 'yes', 'mm' or 'uh huh'.
fillers	Words like 'erm' and 'um', which speakers use to <u>fill gaps</u> while they think about what to say.
formality	How far speech fits in with <u>accepted conventions</u> (particularly <u>Standard English</u>) — e.g. a radio documentary is likely to be <u>more formal</u> than a chat between friends.
idiolect	An <u>individual</u> speaker's unique <u>way of speaking</u>, influenced by their <u>age</u> and <u>background</u>.
interaction	The amount of <u>input</u> from different people and how they <u>act</u> and <u>react</u> to each other.
jargon	<u>Specialist words</u> that relate to a particular <u>job</u> or <u>activity</u>.
micropause	A <u>pause</u> lasting <u>less than a second</u>, that's shown in this book by '<u>(.)</u>' on a transcript.
multi-modal talk	Talk that contains features of both <u>written</u> and <u>spoken</u> language, e.g. <u>text messages</u>.
power	The <u>importance</u> of the people talking to each other — e.g. during a job interview the interviewer holds most of the power.
pragmatics	The <u>meaning behind</u> what a speaker says (e.g. "<u>Well, I'll leave you to it then...</u>" means "<u>I'm leaving</u>"). It makes conversations more <u>polite</u>.
public talk	Language that's written to be <u>spoken</u> to others — e.g. <u>political speeches</u> or <u>presentations</u>.
repertoire	The different <u>ways</u> that a person talks in different <u>situations</u> make up their <u>repertoire</u>, e.g. you might speak differently to a stranger in a shop than to an old friend.
slang	<u>Informal</u> words that are used most in <u>casual conversation</u> and multi-modal talk, e.g. 'cool', 'naff'.
sound representation	How the <u>noises</u> or <u>pronunciation</u> that you'd use during speech are <u>written down</u> — e.g. 'YAAAAYYY', 'woop!!!'.
Standard English	A <u>social dialect</u> of English, used in <u>writing</u> and <u>formal speaking</u>, that's associated with <u>power</u>, <u>education</u> and <u>class</u>. It's what many people think of as '<u>correct</u>' English.
transcript	<u>Spoken language</u> that has been <u>written down</u> so it can be studied.
turn-taking	The <u>behaviour</u> of speakers in a conversation when they <u>let each other speak</u>.
vague language	words or phrases that <u>fill gaps</u> in conversation rather than helping it make sense, e.g. 'sort of', 'like'. Also <u>non-specific words</u> like 'lots' or 'a few'.

Index